Liverpool Life is a dip into the archives of the Liverpool Daily Post and Echo. A scouse time machine that transports us to the land where memory lives.
The images in this collection reflect some part of all of our lives, but in no sense all of any of our lives.
It's a shoebox full of old photographs, the ones you always intended to organise and put in an album, but never got round to.

This collection doesn't pretend to be comprehensive or definitive. It doesn't reflect any individual or section of society. It reflects the many and varied aspects of our lives from childhood to old age.

We guarantee that every reader will find something in these pages that strikes a chord and raises a smile. Through the pages of our Heritage Picture Collections you can keep your past on a bookshelf.

We hope you get as much enjoyment in reading these volumes as we do in producing them.

Above The author, Colin Hunt, aged six.

Playtime arrived at Eldon Place in June 1953. Corporation workers installed climbing bars in the new playground and they were soon in use. The new Elizabethan age may have dawned following the Coronation, but for many children it was still a time of austerity.

Faded photos yellowed with age
Faces trapped upon a page.

A gang of four caught in time
Now grown old like vintage wine.

My old pumps with string for laces,
My best friends with dirty faces.

All those friends from years gone by
Where are they now, and where am I?

Left   Although the act enabling play streets had been passed in 1938 it was May 1948 before these Liverpool youngsters were able to play in safety. By the late 1960s increasing traffic levels had all but finished the play streets. A few lingered on until 1994 when the city council ordered the phasing out of all such streets.

Right   In April 1964 housewives in Monfa Road, Bootle, were so incensed by motorists using the entry at the back of their houses as a "rat run" that they blocked it with their dustbins. For local children it was the opportunity for an impromptu game of "king of the castle".

Boys' toys in 1962. Give it a push and watch it roll. Four little boys take advantage of the slope in a street off Netherfield Road.

An oasis of calm in a busy city. Mother and child in the tranquil beauty of Princes Park.

It's late August and the 1978/79 football season opens in Edge Hill. The pitch is a bit firm and bumpy and the goalposts are bricks, but nothing beats the joy of scoring a goal.

Imagine. Pieces of wood for guitars, but this fab foursome keep the fans entertained at Grenville Street playground in 1970

The carefree days of childhood

Top Getting across Queens Drive at Rice Lane with a pram has never been easy, there has always been plenty of traffic, even in 1968.
Above If babies only knew what a great life they had, maybe they wouldn't cry so much.

It's all well and good being the first family in the street to have a television in the kitchen, but it's a long wait until 1983 when Breakfast TV starts up and there's only Watch with Mother to keep the kids amused on a rainy day.

Top One of the highlights of the summer was dad's work's sports day. This one at the Police Club on Prescot Road shows the boys' sprint, naturally all the lads are dressed in their Sunday best.

Above Families queue at the mobile vaccination unit in West Derby during Liverpool's 1961 anti-polio campaign.

Schooldays are the
happiest days of
our lives.

Discuss.

Top "That boy at the back"... You may know the answer but sometimes it's just too much effort to put your hand up. You let yourself drift into
a dreamworld of footy with your mates, being a rock star and that dark-eyed girl from Notre Dame whose kiss tasted of peppermint.
Above Simple things stimulate young minds at a nursery in 1962.

Civic pride. Well scrubbed pupils at Birchfield Road school receive their illuminated certificates celebrating the 1937 Coronation, from the Lady Mayoress.

An image of childhood innocence. A small boy tries to squeeze on to the end of the wishing seat in the Children's Garden in Stanley Park in 1929.

It looks like the start of an Enid Blyton story. An August day in 1956 at Childwall Cross. Over the wall and down the hill lies Jackson's pond, the scene of pirate adventures on rafts made out of old planks and a great place to collect frog spawn in jam jars.

Sunday best for these two sisters by the boating lake in Sefton Park in July 1965.

Sefton Park was a magnet for families on those summer afternoons of the late Fifties, and what could be nicer than a cool drink at the cafe (top).
A pleasant spring day brings the visitors to Sefton Park's aviary in 1959.

"And the winner of the 1946 Cheshire Lines Station Garden Competition is"...West Derby Station. All thanks to the hard work of Mrs Stevens and Mrs Allen who grew everything from seed.

Regeneration in 1929. The view along Fenwick Street with India Buildings (left) and Martins Bank headquarters starting to take shape. Both buildings were designed by Herbert Rowse who also designed the Queensway Tunnel entrances and ventilation building exteriors, as well as the Philharmonic Hall.

In the post war years when housing was at a premium there were many government inspired self-build schemes. Families like the Thompsons in Huyton take advantage to build their own family home.

Does this count as culture? The man with the iron chest entertains the crowds on Great Charlotte Street in 1946.

Top The, not-so-fully-fitted, kitchen in 1957, with some unsubtle product placement from Omo and Vim.
Above The changing face of Speke in 1938 as the first completed row of corporation housing threatens the traditional cottages across the road.

Top New housing in Bootle's dockland in 1958, and not a single car in sight.
Above Community spirit still in evidence in 1986 in Liverpool's last wash-house, the Fred Robinson Public Laundry in Heyworth Street

November sunshine brings the shoppers to Kirkby market in 1966. Northwood flats stand like sentinels in the background.

Top They built the houses but forgot the shopping centre. Mobile shops were the only amenity in this part of Cantril Farm in 1967.
Above The queue at Cassidy's bakery in Kensington during the December 1974 bread strike

Top The queue outside a Liverpool shop as sweets came off ration on 24 April 1949. The demand was so great and the impact on sugar supplies so significant that the government had to impose rationing again four months later. Sweet rationing which began in July 1942 was not finally lifted until February 1953.

Above The queue at Cassidy's bakery in Kensington during the December 1974 bread strike

It may be 1960 but shopkeeper Wing Lee keeps tradition alive by totting up the bill on his abacus.

On a cold November morning over 1,000 people queued outside Millett's Army and Navy Stores in Church Street for a sale of couponless goods. There were 300 WRNS raincoats, 500 overalls, 50 blankets and 1,000 football jerseys among the goods on offer.

Top   Shoppers wander among the traffic at the junction of County Road and Hale Road in 1958. The Walton Road, County Road stretch had
       claimed the lives of 26 children in the previous year.
Above The record department at Rushworth's may have stocked everything from Bennett to Buddy but it was never as cool as Nems.

What more could anyone want for Christmas in 1962 other than an inflatable Yogi Bear or Huckleberry Hound

The chill wind off the river,
the warmth of the welcome,
the smell of whisky, the laughter
of children, the tears for those
departed, Uncle John asleep in
the parlour, and all before dinner.

Christmas in Liverpool

Top Christmas shoppers pack the narrow pavements on Church Street in 1966.
Above Christmas Eve in St John's Market. The longer you wait the more the price of the turkeys come down in a game of patience with the butcher.

The row of prams parked outside Donaldson Street public laundry were used by the customers to transport their weekly wash.

Time for a natter with neighbours while donkey stoning the front step in China Street in 1965.

Even if he had been wearing a crash helmet this motorcyclist wouldn't have had much protection from a sudden April snowstorm in 1968.

The illuminated weather forecast sign on the Post and Echo building at the corner of Whitechapel and Crosshall Street was a city landmark for nearly twenty years from August 1955.

Commuters arriving at Central Station on the 7.10am from Manchester in 1963.

Top   A chilly journey home for these commuters in January 1961 as they queue in South Castle Street.
Above Uniforms worn with pride as service personnel mingle with passengers coming off the New Brighton boat in 1947.

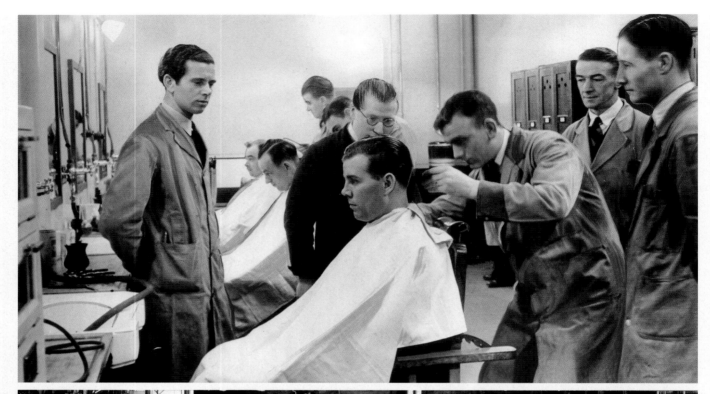

Top Ex-servicemen learn a new trade in men's hairdressing at the Government Vocational Training Centre, Stopgate Lane in November 1945.
Above Life on the line in the re-tread moulding department at Dunlop's in Speke.

The 120ft long Viva gearbox assembly conveyor at Vauxhall's Ellesmere Port plant in 1975.

The words, muffled by the grey blanket of fog are unintelligible, but everyone recognises the tune. "Raa boh, any ole raa boh"
Like a call to prayer for the faithful, the rag and bone man's call hangs in the Liverpool fog in 1976.

"Any more fares please". Service with a smile as bus conductor number CC51245, Len Hughes collects fares in 1965.

Top Clippies at Dingle depot in 1952 receiving instruction in the use of new ticket machines. They already know the drill for the bell. One ring for stop, two rings for go and three rings for a full bus and don't stop to pick up any more passengers.

Above Often forgotten in Merseyside's industrial history, the Triumph Toledo. In 1970 it was the first car assembled at the Triumph factory in Speke, which also manufactured the Dolomite and TR7.

A friendly bobby sees children across busy Scotland Road in the early 1970s, close to the Parrot pub.

The Fifties

The Sixties

Less than ten years separated the 1957 works' dance photograph on the top from the community centre jive picture below, but in that decade the world had changed for ever.

More Number Ones
than any other city.

Need we say more?

Top A glass of Double Diamond and music to dance to on the jukebox, in Stanley House in 1961.
Above The pre-fab four at Allan Williams' Jacaranda Club in February 1959. The Caribbean "All Steel" band are, left to right, Frank Rechek, Talbot "Bones" Thomas, Gary Gobin and Peter "Otts" Gordon.

It was strictly ballroom at the Murphy Dance School show at the Grafton Rooms in May 1959.

Top Gossip and glamour in the ladies at Quadrant Park in 1988.
Above Get up on the dance floor for Eighties' disco, funk and soul at Cagneys.

It may look like shove ha'penny, but coach Alan Hampson is discussing match tactics with his players at Prescot Cables in 1959

Top A sunny Monday afternoon in June 1976 and Lancashire are going well. It beats working.

Above Female fans at football matches are no new phenomenon. Veteran Anfield groundsman Bert Riley chats to the regulars by the players' tunnel, while waiting for the teams to come out for the Liverpool v Wolves FA Cup tie in February 1952.

1966 and all that. Under Oxford's dreaming spires their dreams are of lofty ambition, of high art and matters of politics, but here we dream of scoring in front of the Gwladys or the Kop.

Overcome by the emotion of it all the supplicant grips the silver chalice held by Goodison's high priest, as a sideswoman give comfort.
Harry Catterick comforts Jennifer Jones, who had to be lifted out of the huge crowd during Everton's homecoming celebrating the Blues'
epic victory over Sheffield Wednesday in the 1966 FA Cup Final.

Hi Ho Hi Ho... Not a hard hat or fluorescent jacket in sight on a chill February morning in 1962. Merseyside's last gang of railway linesmen's female assistants, known as lengthwomen, set off to weed and shovel ballast near Meols station, armed with nothing more than headscarves, raincoats and zip up bootees to keep them safe and warm.

It may be boring on the line at Dunlop's footwear plant in Walton, but at least you can come to work in your curlers.

There are only ten years apart in these two photographs but the girls at Millbank College in 1971 **(top)** are a world apart from the students at this Liverpool Secretarial College improving their handwriting to the strains of the Bluebell Polka on the wind-up gramophone.

You may give them jobs to numb the brain as well as the backside, but you can't keep a good woman down. The discipline and control of life in the switchroom at Lancaster House, Liverpool's main telephone exchange, in 1970, contrasts with the laughter in the face of adversity attitude of the women at United Biscuits, (we called it Crawfords), when the factory in Binns Road closed in June 1986.

A woman's work is
never done. . .even
when she gets her P45

Top Now at the heart of the Liverpool One development these gardens between
Paradise Street and South John Street were created on bomb sites in the
Fifties. They were a fantastic lunchtime escape for thousands of office workers.

Above Learning to set the table was high on the list of skills for a domestic goddess
in 1964.

A dozen of Liverpool's finest win through to the semi-final of the 1971 Miss Liverpool Contest. Helen Searle, Elizabeth Home, Geraldine Littler, Patricia Duncan, Patricia Capper, Beryl McMahon, Irene Jenkins, Anita Holder, Cheryl Lewis, Sandra McFaul, Lillian Rodgers and Carol Warburton. Where are you now girls?

Two office girls take a stroll in the September sun in 1956 along Chapel Walk off Castle Street, one of Liverpool's lost by ways.

Top Summer time and the living is easy, but not when your bales of cotton have just fallen into Old Hall Street. Although this is 1974 very little remains of this view except the Waterloo warehouse with its tower (far left). The "Eddies" (the King Edward pub), the warehouses, including Bibby's, and the Northern Hospital (right) have all been consigned to history.

Above This is Cases Street in 1978, once a bustling shortcut between Ranelagh Street and Clayton Square, now reduced to the crowded approach to the shopping centre. Although it boasted a concentration of lively pubs it is best remembered by men of a certain age for Blakes Medical Stores. The spartan window of this surgical appliance dealer was dominated by an illuminated sign promoting Durex. As youthful curiosity gave way to adolescent hopefulness and then mature necessity, the visits to Cases Street became an enduring source of embarrassment for many a young man.

The weary donkey has seen it all before as two young sisters "watch the birdie" on New Brighton beach in July 1955.

Top Passengers board the Crosville for London in St John's Lane in July 1960. In the background the policeman on point duty outside Lime Street Station entrance and the Punch and Judy cafe halts a distinctive Reeces van coming along Lime Street.

Above Crowd shelter under New Brighton pier as a Whit Sunday thunderstorm breaks in 1960.

The passengers leaving the King Orry are well wrapped up against the cold after spending Christmas on the Isle of Man in 1960.

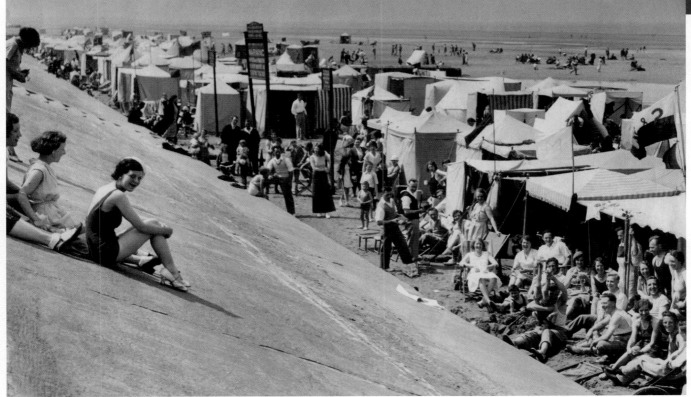

Top A packed Lime Street Station in August 1959 as thousands take their holidays during the main factory weeks..
Above A tented village spreads along the embankment at Harrison Drive in 1934 as holidaymakers make the most of the June sunshine.

Too much monkey business

A massive queue of visitors for the first Sunday opening of Knowsley Hall in June 1949.
By July 1971 the grounds of the Hall had become an altogether more hazardous place, particularly if you were the rear lights on an Austin 1100.
"Anyone got a monkey wrench?"

It could be some rural backwater, but it's Calderstones Park on a summer's afternoon in the Sixties.

Top The Pine Tree Cafe at Freshfield in 1959. Sadly the cafe fell victim to coastal erosion and was wrecked in a storm in October 1961, which caused it to collapse into the sea.

Above On a perfect June day in 1963 the Mersey is like a mill pond. The Elder Dempster liner anchored mid-river is like a painted ship. In the foreground a group of boys find the only patch of short grass on the riverside slopes at Egremont for a game of cricket.

Families enjoy their day out among the litter at the 1972 Liverpool Show.

An old lady looks out across the blighted acres of the city in 1970.

She sees the spectres of her past, the streets where her children played, the homes of friends and neighbours. She hears the echo of her husband's footsteps as he walks home from work and the sound of his laughter as he comes home from the pub. She sees her life reduced to rubble then swept away.

A child knows only what she sees, until she is shown a world without horizons.

A glorious burst of late Autumn sunshine throws shadows across the fallen leaves on Aigburth Drive in October 1951.

Bootle WVS Darby and Joan Club enjoy their Coronation celebration luncheon at the Town Hall in 1953.

Once they sailed the oceans. They survived typhoons in the South China Seas and brawls in New York. They got drunk in Panama and sick in Shanghai.
They brought parrots and monkeys back from Manaus and embarrassing infections back from Marseilles.
In April 1974 they play penny bingo at the Ancient Mariners' Club at the Mersey Mission to Seamen.

Top When we're young and learning about life we need help in climbing the stairs and riding a bike. Sometimes when we're older and nature plays her cruel jokes on our bodies we need help all over again.

Above God's waiting room. Like the doctor's surgery they sit working their way through the magazines that have been there since the dawn of time. Coats on ready for the call. "Next please".

Doesn't matter if you're young or old. You can still push the boat out, like this man and boy at Walton Hall Park boating lake in 1966.

A city with salt water in its veins

In the Fifties the river was such a busy place, there was always something to see. In March 1959 the Carinthia heads for New York **(top)**, while vessels jostle for space at the landing stage in June 1957.

Old friends stand and chat on the corner of Upper Pitt Street, while young friends head back to the Liverpool Institute after a lunchtime trip to the city centre.

You're only as old as you feel. The Wellington pub near Byrom Street in 1980.

A kiss on New Brighton's big wheel at the dawn of the Sixties. A time to be young, a time for hope, a time for change.

Light and shade, an uncertain future, but someone to share it with.
Overleaf The wheel of time turns, and on the bank of an ageless river a grandfather and child complete the circle of life. Rock Ferry 1939